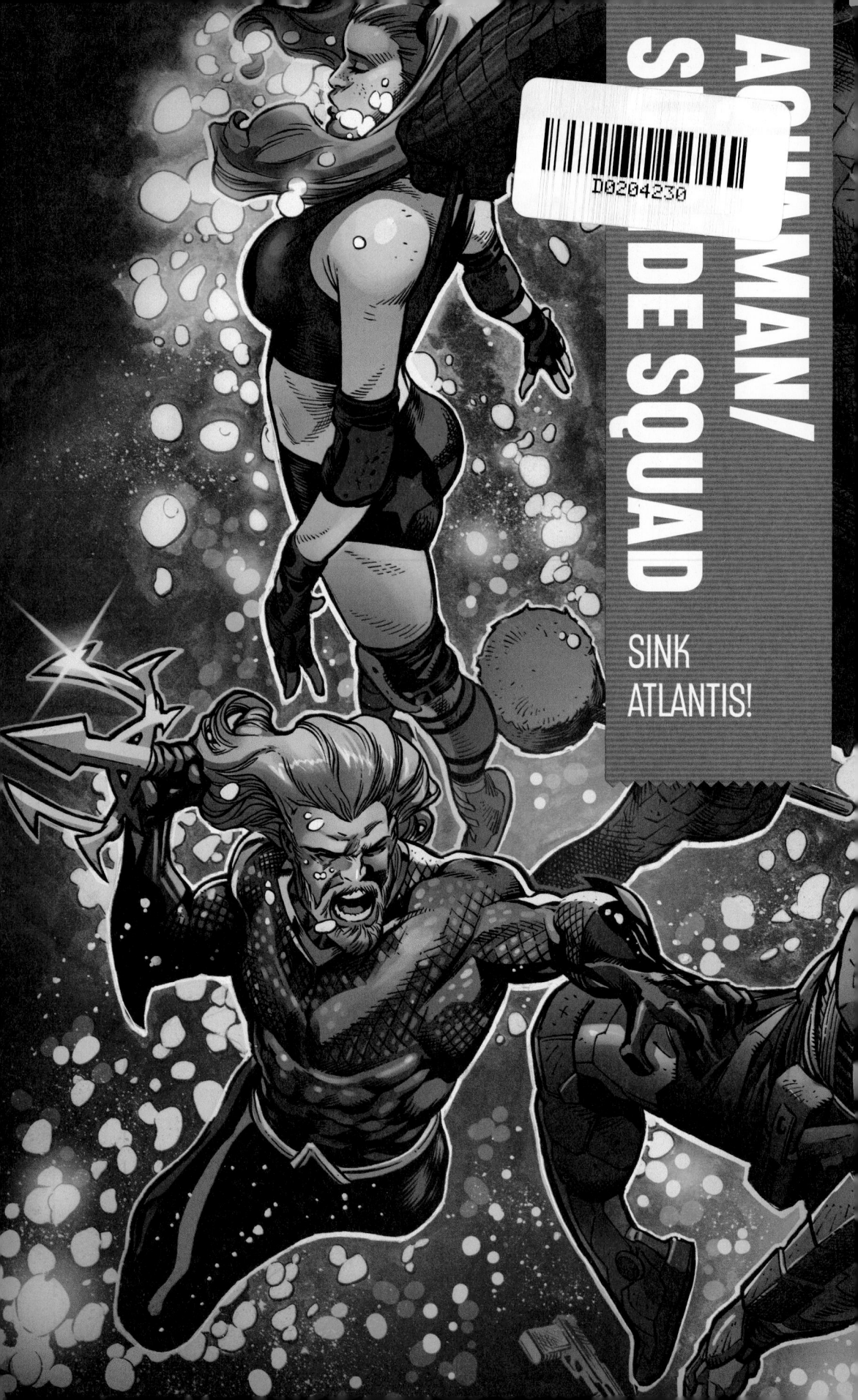

AQUAMAN/ SUICIDE SQUAD

SINK ATLANTIS!

writers

ROB WILLIAMS
DAN ABNETT

pencillers

JOSÉ LUÍS
JOE BENNETT

inkers

JORDI TARRAGONA
VICENTE CIFUENTES

colorist

ADRIANO LUCAS

letterers

PAT BROSSEAU
STEVE WANDS

collection cover artists

RAFA SANDOVAL
and **IVAN PLASCENCIA**

AQUAMAN created by **PAUL NORRIS**

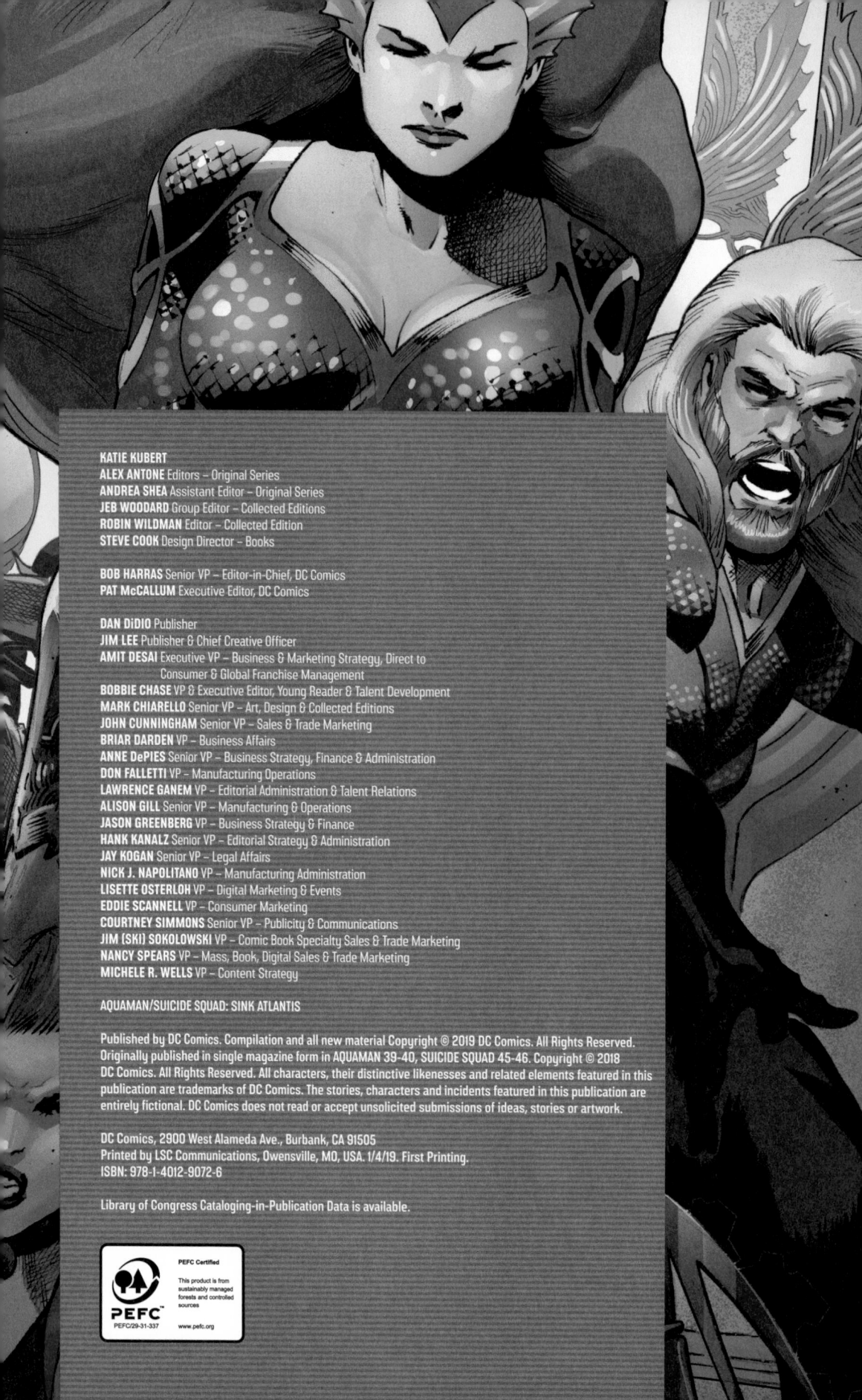

KATIE KUBERT
ALEX ANTONE Editors – Original Series
ANDREA SHEA Assistant Editor – Original Series
JEB WOODARD Group Editor – Collected Editions
ROBIN WILDMAN Editor – Collected Edition
STEVE COOK Design Director – Books

BOB HARRAS Senior VP – Editor-in-Chief, DC Comics
PAT McCALLUM Executive Editor, DC Comics

DAN DiDIO Publisher
JIM LEE Publisher & Chief Creative Officer
AMIT DESAI Executive VP – Business & Marketing Strategy, Direct to
                Consumer & Global Franchise Management
BOBBIE CHASE VP & Executive Editor, Young Reader & Talent Development
MARK CHIARELLO Senior VP – Art, Design & Collected Editions
JOHN CUNNINGHAM Senior VP – Sales & Trade Marketing
BRIAR DARDEN VP – Business Affairs
ANNE DePIES Senior VP – Business Strategy, Finance & Administration
DON FALLETTI VP – Manufacturing Operations
LAWRENCE GANEM VP – Editorial Administration & Talent Relations
ALISON GILL Senior VP – Manufacturing & Operations
JASON GREENBERG VP – Business Strategy & Finance
HANK KANALZ Senior VP – Editorial Strategy & Administration
JAY KOGAN Senior VP – Legal Affairs
NICK J. NAPOLITANO VP – Manufacturing Administration
LISETTE OSTERLOH VP – Digital Marketing & Events
EDDIE SCANNELL VP – Consumer Marketing
COURTNEY SIMMONS Senior VP – Publicity & Communications
JIM (SKI) SOKOLOWSKI VP – Comic Book Specialty Sales & Trade Marketing
NANCY SPEARS VP – Mass, Book, Digital Sales & Trade Marketing
MICHELE R. WELLS VP – Content Strategy

AQUAMAN/SUICIDE SQUAD: SINK ATLANTIS

DC Comics, 2900 West Alameda Ave., Burbank, CA 91505
Printed by LSC Communications, Owensville, MO, USA. 1/4/19. First Printing.
ISBN: 978-1-4012-9072-6

Library of Congress Cataloging-in-Publication Data is available.

SUICIDE SQUAD

#45

...AND LO! ATLANTIS HAS RISEN!

SINK ATLANTIS!

PART ONE

STORY: ROB WILLIAMS AND DAN ABNETT   SCRIPT: ROB WILLIAMS   PENCILS: JOSÉ LUÍS
INKS: JORDI TARRAGONA AND VICENTE CIFUENTES   COLORS: ADRIANO LUCAS
LETTERS: PAT BROSSEAU
COVER: RAFA SANDOVAL, JORDI TARRAGONA AND IVAN PLASCENCIA
ASSISTANT EDITOR: ANDREA SHEA
EDITORS: KATIE KUBERT AND ALEX ANTONE   GROUP EDITOR: BRIAN CUNNINGHAM

"...NO MATTER WHAT."

WASHINGTON, D.C.

ARE YOU *INSANE?*

THEY JUST APPEARED IN THE ATLANTIC--*PRACTICALLY ON OUR DOORSTEP*--AND HAVE MADE NO MOVE TO RETREAT!

THEY SAY THEY *CAN'T.*

I *DON'T GIVE A RAT'S ASS.*

THEY'RE A FOREIGN NATION THAT JUST INVADED AND SENT HIGHLY DESTRUCTIVE TIDAL WAVES INTO *OUR* TERRITORY.

AND WE'RE JUST GOING TO, WHAT? WAVE AT THEM AND ASK HOW WE CAN HELP?

ADMIRAL MEDDINGHOUSE. WE HAVE GOOD COMMUNICATION CHANNELS WITH ATLANTIS, AND WE HAVE *ZERO* INTEREST IN ANGERING A NATION WITH AN ARMY OF DAMN *SEA MONSTERS.*

WE'LL KEEP DIPLOMATIC CHANNELS OPEN AND SEND OUR AMBASSADOR TO THE UPCOMING *ATLANTEAN CORONATION* AS PLANNED.

THEY JUST APPEARED WITHIN DIRECT STRIKING DISTANCE OF US AND NOW THEY'RE CROWNING THEIR *QUEEN?*

ATLANTIS IS A *MAJOR* THREAT TO THE UNITED STATES. MY FEELINGS ON THIS ARE WELL-KNOWN. AS IS MY PRIOR EXPERIENCE WITH THE ATLANTEANS.*

*BACK IN AQUAMAN VOL. 2: BLACK MANTA RISING.

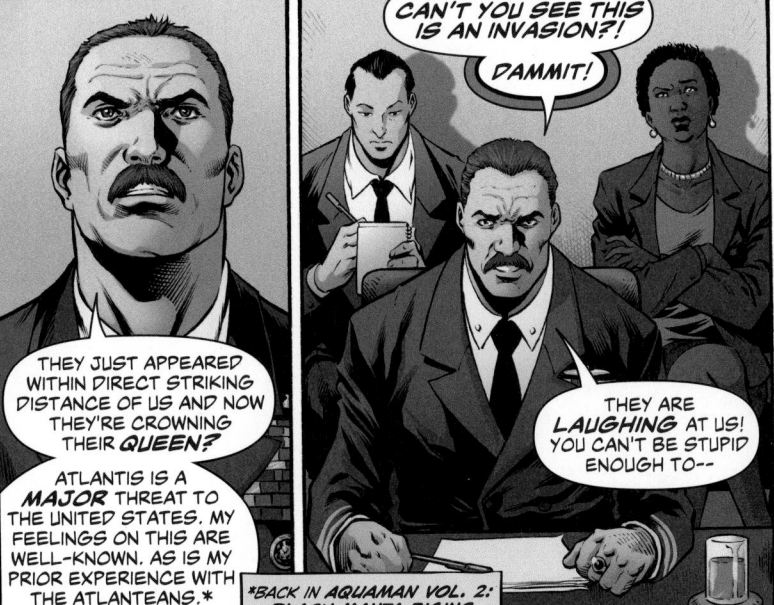

CAN'T YOU SEE THIS IS AN INVASION?!

DAMMIT!

THEY ARE *LAUGHING* AT US! YOU CAN'T BE STUPID ENOUGH TO--

THAT IS THE **PRESIDENT'S** POSITION, ADMIRAL.

PERHAPS YOU WOULD LIKE TO INFORM HIM THAT YOU FEEL HIS POSITION IS **STUPID**.

THIS BRIEFING IS OVER, GENTLEMEN.

... YES, MR. SECRETARY.

BELLE REVE, DO YOU HEAR ME?

READING YOU, DIRECTOR WALLER.

MEETING JUST ENDED. RETURNING TO THE PENITENTIARY SHORTLY. HAVE KATANA PREP THE **ENCHANTRESS REPLACEMENT**--

AMANDA...

...A WORD.

MEET MY NEWEST ASSET--KNOWN AS *LORD SATANIS.*

HEY, FLOYD? DID THIS GUY SAY HIS NAME WAS "SATIN ANUS"?

WHAT HE'S CARRYING HERE IS A MAGICAL PAYLOAD PUT TOGETHER BY OUR TECH PEOPLE. IT WILL REVERSE THE EFFECTS OF THE MAGIC THAT "RAISED" ATLANTIS, KEEPING CASUALTIES TO A MINIMUM.

ISN'T THAT *RIGHT?*

HEAR ME, WOMAN... SATANIS DOES NOT BELONG WITH SCUM LIKE THEM...SATANIS WILL STRIP THE *FLESH OFF YOUR BONES.*

SATANIS WILL--

I THINK SO, HARL. WELCOME TO THE SUICIDE SQUAD, PAL.

YOU DARE--!

STAY *PUT,* SATANIS. OR I BLOW THE BOMB THAT'S IN YOUR BRAIN.

THE BOMB THAT IS IN *ALL OF YOUR* BRAINS, IN CASE YOU FORGOT.

YOUR TARGET IS THE *SILENT SCHOOL,* DEEP IN THE HEART OF ATLANTIS. IT'S STILL SUBMERGED BENEATH THE CITY. ONE OF THE MOST *SECURE* FACILITIES IN THE WORLD.

YOU BREAK IN AND PLANT THE MAGICAL DEVICE.

ATLANTIS WILL SINK.

QUESTION! IF THIS PLACE IS SO SECURE, HOW ARE WE SUPPOSED TA GET IN?

AQUAMAN
#39

The Throne of Atlantis.

SINK ATLANTIS!

PART TWO

STORY: **DAN ABNETT** AND **ROB WILLIAMS** SCRIPT: **DAN ABNETT**
PENCILS: **JOE BENNETT** INKS: **VICENTE CIFUENTES** COLORS: **ADRIANO LUCAS**
LETTERS: **STEVE WANDS** COVER: **RAFA SANDOVAL** AND **IVAN PLASCENCIA**
ASSISTANT EDITOR: **ANDREA SHEA** EDITORS: **ALEX ANTONE** AND **KATIE KUBERT**
GROUP EDITOR: **BRIAN CUNNINGHAM**

"...*PLEASE* FIND OUT WHERE THE HELL ARTHUR IS."

Security Watch Station, Atlantis.

ARE YOU BUSY, MURK?

SUICIDE SQUAD

#46

ATLANTIS.
MID-ATLANTIC.

"ONE THING DR. QUINZEL, SEXY PSYCHIATRIST AN' PhD, WORKED OUT LONG AGO? THERE'S A LOT MORE GOING ON BELOW THE SURFACE A' MOST PEOPLE.

"..."

"I'M SURE THERE'S A METAPHOR FOR ATLANTIS AROUND HERE SOMEWHERE...

"...BUT I DIGRESS! ATLANTIS HAS RISEN. SOME OF IT, ANYWAY. SOMEBODY HIGH UP IN THE UNITED STATES GOVERNMENT-- NOT VERY HAPPY ABOUT IT!

"THE SUICIDE SQUAD IS SNEAKILY SENT IN TO DELIVER A *PACKAGE* TO ATLANTIS' LOWER LEVELS.

"THIS WILL, WE'RE TOLD, SEND ATLANTIS BACK TO THE BOTTOM OF THE OCEAN, WHERE IT BELONGS.

BUT-- *SHOCK TWIST*--WE FIND OUT THE PACKAGE IS REALLY JUST'A BIG-ASS NUKE.

SOME OF US SQUAD FOLK ARE *NOT* COOL ABOUT BLOWING UP AN ENTIRE CITY OF CIVILIAN FISH-FOLK. A VIGOROUS INTERNAL DISAGREEMENT FOLLOWS.

DEADSHOT AND I GET CAPTURED IN THE MELEE AND...

OH...

...

WAS I SAYING ALL THAT OUT LOUD?

HEY, DEADSHOT, HOW LONG HAVE THESE GUYS BEEN THERE LISTENING? OUT OF INTEREST.

THE WHOLE TIME, HARL.

OOPS.

MURK. COMMANDER OF THE DRIFT.

I WAS WILLING TO HAVE YOU TORTURED IN ORDER TO UNCOVER YOUR PLAN. I THANK YOU FOR SAVING ME THE MORAL QUANDARY.

THE DRY-MOUTHS ARE GETTING STUPIDER AND STUPIDER.

NOT ALL OF US, PAL. JUST THE CRAZY ONES.

I RESEMBLE THAT.

LOOK, WE AIN'T NO HEROES, BUT WE DRAW THE LINE AT KILLING KIDS. *I* DRAW THAT LINE.

TALK, INTERLOPER! WHERE ARE YOUR COMPANIONS--

THE SILENT SCHOOL.

OOPS! I DID IT AGAIN.

AT LEAST I DIDN'T TELL YOU MY SUPER-SECRET MISSION WALLER HERSELF GAVE ME--

WHAT SECRET MISSION? TALK!

OW!

CHILLAX, FISH BREATH!

I'VE GOT THE *WORST* MEMORY, SO I WROTE IT ON MY ARM, 'KAY?

STORY ROB WILLIAMS AND DAN ABNETT SCRIPT ROB WILLIAMS PENCILS JOSE LUIS
INKS JORDI TARRAGONA COLORS ADRIANO LUCAS LETTERS PAT BROSSEAU
COVER RAFA SANDOVAL, JORDI TARRAGONA AND IVAN PLASCENCIA ASSISTANT EDITOR ANDREA SHEA
EDITORS KATIE KUBERT AND ALEX ANTONE GROUP EDITOR BRIAN CUNNINGHAM

I WOULD VERY MUCH LIKE YOUR COUNTRY TO BE A GREAT FRIEND TO ATLANTIS.

A FEELING WE VERY MUCH RECIPROCATE.

WHAT? I...I ASSURE YOU...THIS HAS NOTHING TO DO WITH THE U.S. GOVERNMENT.

PERHAPS. PERHAPS NOT.

EXACTLY WHO ORDERED THIS PREEMPTIVE STRIKE AGAINST US IS NOT CLEAR.

BUT THIS MUCH *IS* CLEAR.

I HAVE ORDERED THE VERY SEAS SURROUNDING YOUR NATION TO RISE UP AND HOLD FOR MY INSTRUCTIONS. MY ARMIES, CONTAINING HORRORS YOU CANNOT EVEN BEGIN TO IMAGINE, AWAIT WITHIN THOSE WAVES.

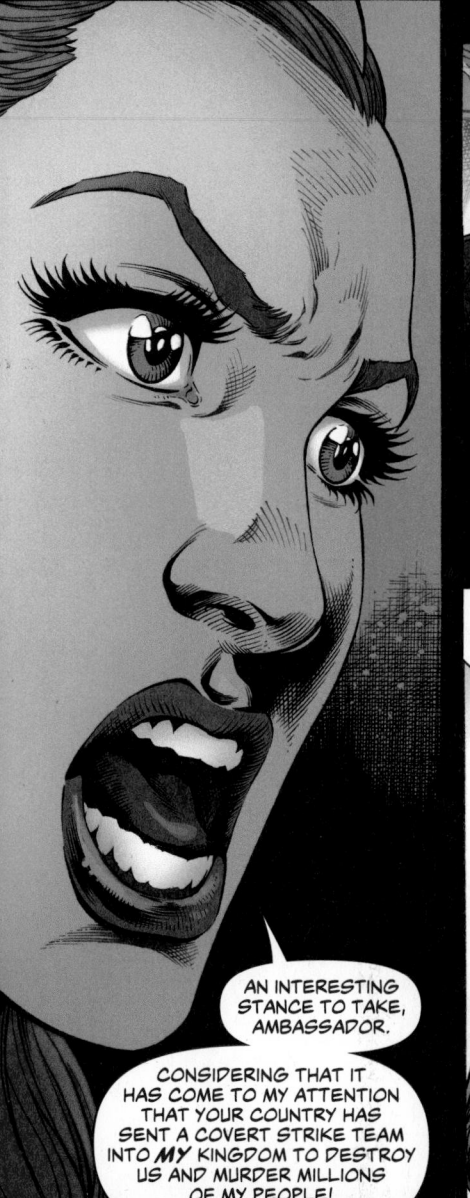

AN INTERESTING STANCE TO TAKE, AMBASSADOR.

CONSIDERING THAT IT HAS COME TO MY ATTENTION THAT YOUR COUNTRY HAS SENT A COVERT STRIKE TEAM INTO *MY* KINGDOM TO DESTROY US AND MURDER MILLIONS OF MY PEOPLE!

TO SPEAK PLAINLY, AMBASSADOR...

AQUAMAN
#40

VARIANT COVER GALLERY

SUICIDE SQUAD #45 variant cover
By EMANUELA LUPACCHINO and DAVE MCCAIG

SUICIDE SQUAD #46 variant cover
By FRANCESCO MATTINA

AQUAMAN #40 variant cover
By JOSHUA MIDDLETON

"AQUAMAN has been a rollicking good ride so far... The mythology Johns has been building up here keeps getting teased out at just the right rate, like giving a junkie their fix." **– MTV GEEK**

"With Reis on art and Johns using his full creative juices, AQUAMAN is constantly setting the bar higher and higher." **– CRAVE ONLINE**

AQUAMAN
VOL. 1: THE TRENCH
GEOFF JOHNS
with IVAN REIS

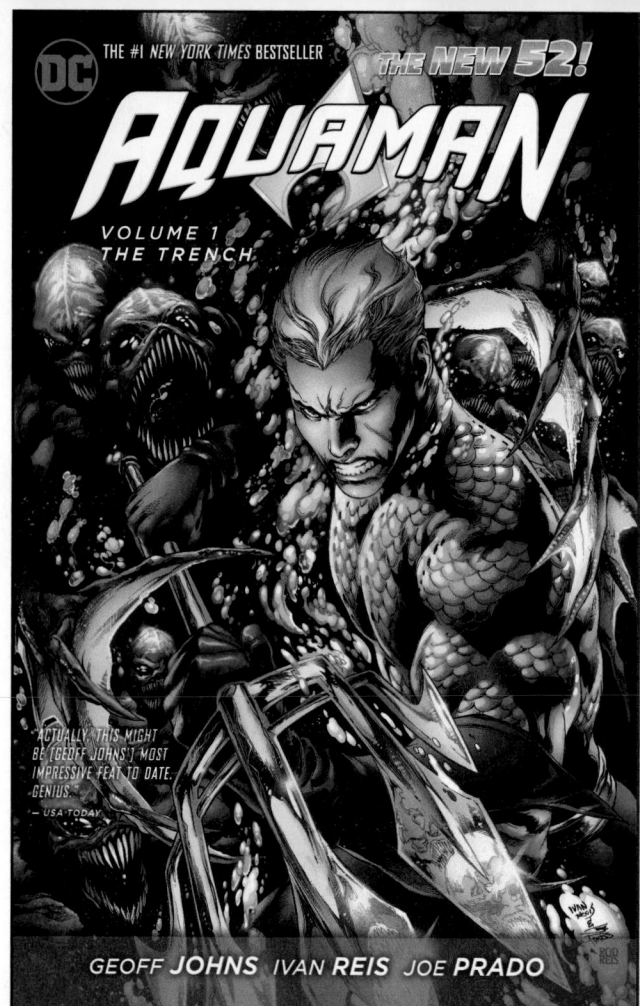

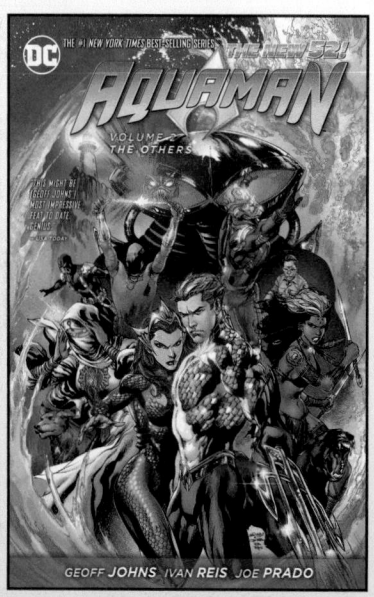

AQUAMAN VOL. 2:
THE OTHERS

AQUAMAN VOL. 3:
THRONE OF ATLANTIS

READ THE ENTIRE EPIC!

AQUAMAN VOL. 4:
DEATH OF A KING

AQUAMAN VOL. 5:
SEA OF STORMS

AQUAMAN VOL. 6:
MAELSTROM

AQUAMAN VOL. 7:
EXILED

AQUAMAN VOL. 8:
OUT OF DARKNESS

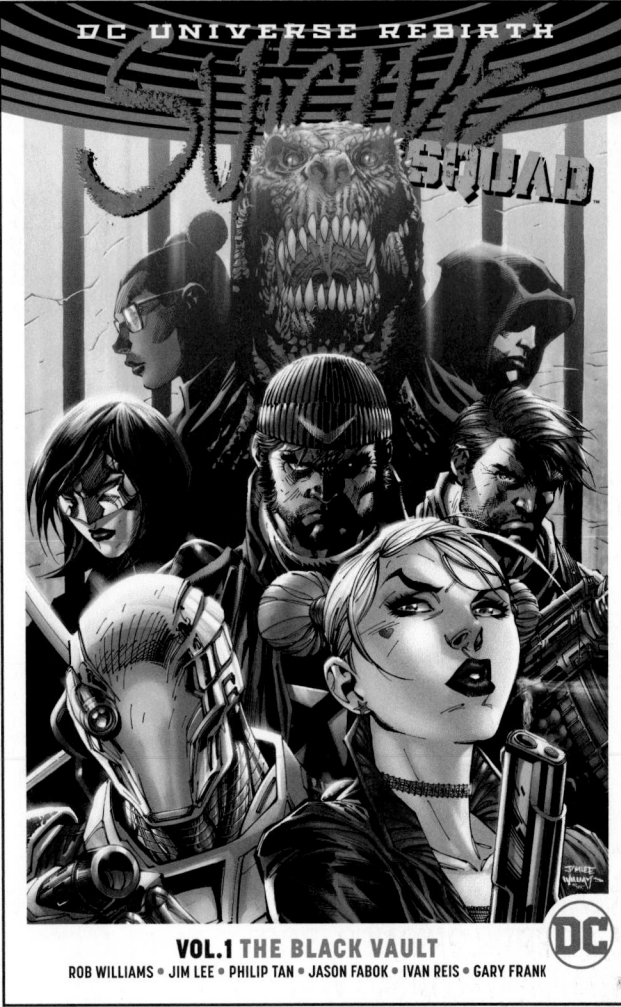

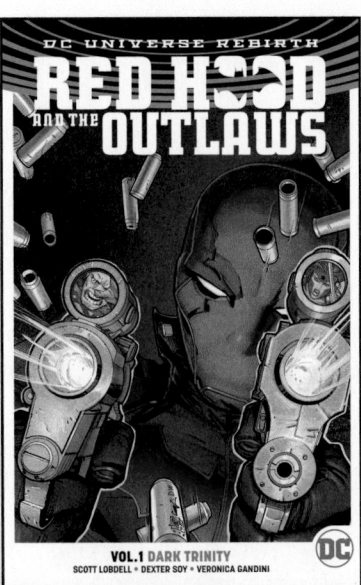

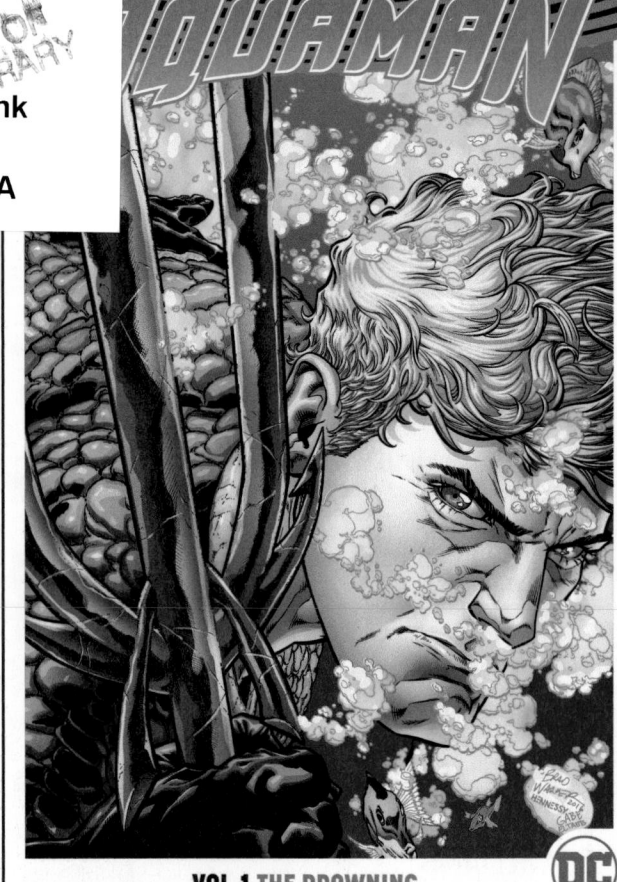

"All aboard for AQUAMAN!"
–NERDIST

"A solid primer on Aquaman's new status quo."
–COMIC BOOK RESOURCES

AQUAMAN
VOL. 1: THE DROWNING

DAN ABNETT with
PHILIPPE BRIONES, SCOT
EATON and BRAD WALKER

READ THE ENTIRE EPIC!

AQUAMAN VOL. 4:
UNDERWORLD

AQUAMAN VOL. 5:
THE CROWN COMES DOWN

AQUAMAN VOL. 2:
BLACK MANTA RISING

AQUAMAN VOL. 3:
CROWN OF ATLANTIS